Bathed by Rainbows

An anthology of poetry and prose from 'Land, Sea, Sky, Self' and 'Magic Words', two series of creative writing for wellbeing sessions at The Hub, Port Erin, Isle of Man.

Edited by Janet Lees

ISBN 978-0-359-92133-1

Cover image copyright © Janet Lees
Cover design by Ian Pilbeam

published by dpdotcom publishing

Acknowledgements

With grateful thanks to Year of Our Island for kindly supporting the two series of workshops that inspired this anthology, and to Isle of Man Arts Council for their generous support of creative writing for wellbeing at The Hub since 2014.

Thanks to Boakesey for the anthology title, which comes from her piece 'The Respite of Dreams', on page 14.

Contents

Acknowledgements   5

Contents   7

Foreword   9

Introduction   11

Prose and poetry by:

Boakesey   13

Angela Callister   19

Shirley Corlett   21

Ron Couch   29

Candice Jones   34

Giselle Marks   36

Jaya Martin   39

Anna Mercer   46

Christine Pollard   49

Grainney Sheard   50

Gill Stephens   51

Debra Tracey   54

Foreword

I am absolutely delighted to be writing this foreword to the second Hub anthology. Perhaps I will start with a few sentences about Janet Lees, the creative writing for wellbeing facilitator, because without her expert guidance this anthology would never have been.

When we were setting up the Hub in Port Erin in 2011 it was a daunting task. There was no blueprint to follow other than the remit that we wanted to create a place for the community that would help alleviate isolation and loneliness. A place where people could come and join in with different activities, or just be. Back then I had no idea of the benefits of creativity to wellbeing – I had so much to learn.

I was discussing this with Janet, whom I had met professionally some years previously and she tentatively suggested doing some creative writing sessions on the premise that this would bring people together in a warm, welcoming and safe environment where they could learn some skills and express themselves.

I was hooked. I knew Janet had recently completed her MA in Creative Writing – soon to be followed by specific training in Writing for Wellbeing – and I'd been intrigued by her workshop experiences. And so we began...

Since those early days I've always look forward to the writing sessions, as I know they bring together an eclectic group of people who laugh and shed a few tears together while producing the most amazing poetry and prose – often surprising themselves. This anthology is home to some of the compelling and varied work resulting from the sessions, written by a group of wonderful writers, facilitated by an amazing poet and artist.

And the real beauty is that you too could be part of such a group because – like so many of the participants before they came and gave it a go – I bet you're a poet and don't even know it!

Janet Bridle
Southern Community Initiatives Hub Coordinator

Introduction

The Hub has been home to creative writing for wellbeing sessions for the last five years, thanks to generous annual support from the Isle of Man Arts Council. Last year we were also grateful to Year of Our Island, who funded two special series of workshops in which we took inspiration from the Isle of Man.

In the first series of sessions, 'Land, Sea, Sky, Self', our focus was our stunning natural environment in the island, along with our own inner landscapes. In the second series, 'Magic Words', we took inspiration from Manx folklore, history and customs, and explored how some of these things reflect aspects of ourselves.

We imagined ourselves as different people, different creatures, different aspects of the land and the sea. We wrote in praise of the night sky – the island being home to some of the best 'dark sky' sites in the world. We listened to ancient and modern Manx songs, poems and stories, and were transported into the realm of folklore, where magic is as much a part of everyday life as breathing. We wrote poems of gratitude for the people who make our lives special. We wrote about ourselves: our remembered past, our sometimes challenging present, our imagined future. We took inspiration from traditional rituals and dreamed up contemporary ones, brought new-born fairy tales into the world, saw life from the point of view of the fox, the dandelion clock, a mountain in winter. We laughed, and sometimes we cried, as we talked about our fears, our dreams and all the other things that make us human.

Having been hosting creative writing for wellbeing sessions like these for several years, I have an unshakeable belief in the power of creativity to transform. I have this belief because I see it happening again and again. I think of the sessions as mini-breaks for the imagination, two-hour vacations from our everyday lives, giving us the chance to go somewhere completely different – to go wherever we'd like to go.

This ability to travel through time and space does us the power of good. Creative writing sparks explosions of feel-good chemicals because it sets us free. In a group, when you get to share your words with others, it's quietly transformational. Because it's real. It's totally absorbing, it's as unique as you are, and it enables you to connect, in a true way, with others.

The writing you'll read in the following pages represents a range of different voices, all of them distinctive and compelling, alive and shimmering with different emotions and experience, some imagined, some real, some a mixture of both.

Thanks once again to Year of Our Island for enabling these voices to be heard. Thanks to all the Hub creative writers who have generously shared their work in this anthology. And thanks to you, the reader, for being part of it too.

Janet Lees
Creative writing for wellbeing session facilitator

BOAKESEY

Skyku
(Haiku for the sky)

Sentry of the sky
Dark or reddish colours
Uniforms for clouds

Amboseli skies
Unbroken band of star-shine
Girdling the planet

Trying to view the stars
Jurby Prison blocks the light
Stop feeding the meter

The Respite of Dreams

I'm an ancient rocky outcrop, falling sheer down to the sea.
I'm sure you've heard of me; you know me as 'The Chasms'.

My dreams are nearly silent, unlike my waking existence.

My consciousness consists of near constant war, conflict and chaos
as the elements conspire to batter me into nothingness. Why? I
don't know. I've never done anything to annoy the wind, the sea, the
cold, so why punish me in this way? Why do I exist if I'm only fit for
destruction?

All I experience is constant depletion and damage. Rock itself (my
very essence), not to mention plants, insects, larger animals, even
the big two-legs are sometimes destroyed.

Oh and the NOISE – it drives me mad! Why won't it ever stop?

Waves thundering and crashing, wind howling, parts of me
screaming as they're torn off me to tumble down to the merciless
sea below. All day, every day and night. Don't know how I manage
to get any sleep at all. Gulls and crows set my stones on edge with
their cacophonous calling. It's quite unbearable, you know. Even
that flaming blackbird – I'm going to give him 'cheep, cheep' one of
these days. At least you two-legs can go somewhere else and escape
the torment.

Is my whole being to be tortured forever before finally being
eliminated?

So I dream.

Instead of being pummelled and pounded I dream of being gently
soothed by the fresh rains of summer during a rainbow. Each
rainbow is captured fleetingly, imprisoned in a single raindrop. I'm
bathed by rainbows until my minerals gleam with gentle caresses.

I'm still being eroded, but it doesn't hurt as much. Kind destruction,
not the violent devastation of reality. If the land must be lessened

and I must cease to be, let it be slow and gentle, not fierce and brutal.

An oystercatcher once told me that all the broken bits of me get broken down and down into smaller and smaller pieces, which saddens me, but she also said that Nature then joins them all together again to make new rock. Reincarnation? Can't see it myself.

Once I'm gone, that'll be it.

So back to my dreams, my one aspect of sanity in this insane tumult. I talk to the wind who tells me of 'Inland', a place far away from the coastal chaos. I dream of being there, on a gentle, rolling hill rather than a craggy mountain.

Undulating slopes clothed in sensuous grasses and trees. No trees ever stand a chance of growing on my real self, but in dreams anything is possible, so conifers, birch, ash and elm all find succour on my slopes. A mighty oak tree rules the wood, standing high on the topmost peak of my dreamland self, providing shelter to myriad birds I'll never see in reality.

I smell the distinct piney warmth of the conifers, the pollen of the grasses makes me sneeze and then the glorious aromas of flowers in my lower meadow makes me dizzy with delight. And the NOISE has gone. At dream-night, only a gentle breeze reaches my ears. It's not disturbing, rather it acts as a lullaby, snuggling me, blanketing my dreams in whispers. Dream-days fill me with birdsong and the soothing chirruping of insects, whilst the chitter-chatter of small mammals adds laughter to my universe. I can even hear the grass swaying, the flitter-flutter of wings and the burbling crunch of rabbits chewing their food. The sunshine is never too bright, it's like a warm spring or late summer's day and everything is calm and in moderation. Absolute perfection.

Sometimes I dream of gentle storms, silent thunder, spectacular lightning and waves that break upon me without anger or destructive malice. Even hailstorms and snow can be pleasant in my Dreamworld. Did you know that snowfall has its own, special sound? It's never silent. Listen carefully, next time it snows and you'll hear it. I've only heard it in my dreams, but it's quite magical. Then, when it freezes the Dreamworld is transformed into crystal citadels of ice.

But not in *my* world. Reality strikes hard when I awaken. I'm back amidst the never-ending maelstrom. As in some everlasting purgatory, I'm trapped forever, apart from the respite of my dreams and the irresistible draw of extinction.

But you, dear Reader, you have two-legs and a future.
Dream your dreams, as I do. Explore your possibilities.
Nothing is impossible in the Dreamworld.

Then *use* your two-legs and that brain you have.
Walk away from tumult, don't endure it. Don't allow yourself to be destroyed.

Dream your dreams, then visit me and tell me all your troubles.
Leave them with me in my Dreamworld.

Then go to your reality.

And make your dreams come true.

Nearly Free

That's me. The elephant's child
according to my Mum at least –
was she a heffalump?
Seeking knowledge, always
asking questions.
Getting into trouble
Prophetically.

But me. Real me.
I wanted to be
an eagle.
Soaring in the wind
over the stormy
azure sea, defying
ozone-releasing thunder,
as purple moonshine bathes
the frosty ground
in magenta.

Swooping down near
the waterfall – not too close.
Plummeting swiftly
accurately navigating
the confines of the ravine
to grasp my prey.
Perched high on a crag
to survey my domain
to succour my soul
and eat.

It wasn't to be.
Not yet, anyway. Instead
I model myself
on the cat.
I sleep. I eat.
I listen to birdsong.
I sleep again.

Occasionally stirring
myself,
to become, again,
myself.
Jupiter.
Bringer of Joy.
And nearly free.

ANGELA CALLISTER

If the sea was to fly

What if
The bruised old girl
Just left,
Deserted brood agape, her
Undies torn, her
Salty nightie hoisted to the skies?

The whales shall rise on shipwrecked masts, their
Great lungs bellowing at the clouds.
Mackerel lakes shall glitter in the sun.
The seals shall feast on cats.

Should the sea fly, you are advised:
Stay inside.
Line your doors.
Put greaseproof paper on your floors.
Sip air through straws.

My friend, the sea
Disgraced on Look Northwest.
She's done it now, she's bared a breast.

I stand on the bridge.
The sea stares me in the eye.
Just for today, I will not try.

New Year's Eve 2018

A seed grows, or fails.
It sprouts and thrives, or dies.
I thrived.
Each choice I made
Became a twig, became a branch
Became a bough.
Let me stand back and view this tree
Of choices unmade, paths not taken, other mes.
I could have been less scared to fail; tried more,
Completed what I'd started, travelled far,
But I came back.
I folded early, took the easy way -
which turned out to be hard and raw and real -
And I stand here and thank myself
For all those paths not taken,
Every thwarted plan, each wish left unfulfilled,
Because they've brought me here,
To this life, with food and love
And shelter, all luxuries for some
But not for me.
This hard-won fruit is mine, and yet
Too near to see - until I stand
And peer
at my gnarled journey
on the passing of the year.

SHIRLEY CORLETT

Melusine

The waterfall cascaded unceasingly into the vast dark lake and a dense mist blanketed the surface, muffling the sounds of the water flowing downstream. The air was rich with the scent of wild garlic and its flowers gleamed like pearls in the moonlight. The shriek of a barn owl broke the silence before it glided like a ghost towards the trees, hunting for prey.

Into this tranquil place came a man, walking slowly as if in a dream, each step an effort. Near the waterfall was a large rock and, when it was reached, the man sank down upon it, his head and broad shoulders bowed. He looked down at his hands which were large and covered in mud, his right palm blistered. He leant forward to wash his hands in the lake and as he did so, a movement nearby caught his attention. A dark shadow materialised from behind the waterfall, tall and slender. The man tensed, sensing danger, and stood wiping his hands on his trousers, leaving streaks of water and mud behind. All he could make out was a tall figure wrapped in a cloak of rags but then the moon emerged from behind a cloud and the cloak shimmered in a myriad of translucent blues, greens and greys.

"Welcome, John!" a woman's voice called softly, as she pushed back the hood of her cloak to reveal long pale blond hair curling softly to her waist.

"Who are you and how do you know my name?" replied John guardedly.

"I know you well John," she answered. "I have many names, but you may call me Melusine."

John watched Melusine carefully as she approached him. "I do not know you and you have still not told me how you know me!"

Melusine smiled. "Your wife visits me here and has told me all about you," she explained.

Tears filled John's eyes. "My wife is dead!" he cried bitterly. "I have just buried her, her and the babe!"

"I know," said Melusine gently.

"How do you know?" snapped John.

21

"Linnet knew she would not survive the birth. She loved you so much John and cherished the time she had with you."

"I don't understand," John replied. "What do you mean?"

Melusine took his hand. "Sit, John, and I will explain," she said, pulling him down to sit on the rock with her. Brushing the tears from his eyes, John sat without resistance and contemplated the stranger in front of him.

Under her cloak, Melusine wore a silver dress with a moonstone belt and a silver necklace also adorned with moonstones. Her hair was ornamented with silver which reflected the moonlight. She had the fairest skin he had ever seen, unmarked, otherworldly. He could not tell how old she was – she could have been twenty or fifty, but her grey-green eyes held his brown ones and he was transfixed; he felt he was drowning in those eyes, unable to escape.

The story she told was one of deepest sadness; how a young woman had fallen in love with stranger, not from her world. She had tried to resist, knowing that there could be no happy ending for her or her beloved, but life held no meaning for her without him. Seeing how miserable she was, her family reluctantly let her go to him, although they stayed in touch every month. Three years passed and she was happy with her life, but then she became pregnant. Whilst her beloved looked forward to the birth of their child, she knew that that neither she nor the child would survive. Three days ago, when the moon was full, she came to the lake to bid farewell to her family.

"But who are her family?" asked John. "Linnet told me she had none, and the nearest village is many miles from here."

"I am her family," said Melusine. "I am her mother."

"You? Where do you live and why have I never met you before?" John demanded.

"We are not like you, we do not live in cottages as you do," she replied. "Linnet could not explain our life to you while she was alive but she wanted you to understand. I would like to show you where we live and, now that Linnet is gone and there is nothing left for you here, you may come and live with us if you wish."

"I cannot leave, my home is here and Linnet is here. I cannot leave her all alone in the forest, I need to tend her grave."

"Linnet has the babe to keep her company; you have no one. Come with me and I will show you where she grew up and you can meet her sisters. You could have a life with us, not what you are used to perhaps, but at least you would not be alone."

Melusine stood and, taking John's hand, dove into the lake, pulling him with her. Down and down they went into the dark lake and John soon realised that he needed air and started to panic, thrashing about to free himself from Melusine's grip. But Melusine's hand held fast to his wrist and he could not escape. *She is trying to kill me – this is her revenge for Linnet,* he thought. When he could hold his breath no longer, he stopped fighting Melusine and accepted his fate but instead of drowning, he found he could breathe!

Amazed by his survival, John was fascinated that an eerie light encircled them, enabling John to see the weeds and fish surrounding them. Suddenly, there was movement to their left and, as they slowed, into focus came two beings: half human, half fish – mermaids! Astonished, John turned to Melusine only to find that while the moonstones were still around her neck and waist, in place of her dress and cloak she had a beautiful tail.

The mermaids, who Melusine introduced as Linnet's sisters, did not speak in the normal way but John could 'hear' their questions in his head. He found he could respond to them merely by thinking his response. The two sisters welcomed John and took him to their home where they lived with Melusine; a cave deep under the waterfall decorated with items which could only have come from John's homeland. Melusine explained that land dwellers would visit the lake and make offerings to the mermaids in the hope of having a healthy child. This explanation reminded John of Linnet and brought tears to his eyes once more and he felt that, if he stayed, his tears would turn the fresh water lake into to a salty sea. Melusine felt John's pain and knew that he was not ready to remain with them. Farewells were 'said', then they turned and headed back to the waterfall.

When John heard Melusine call his name, he found he was sitting on the rock by the lake, his clothes dry, while Melusine was clothed once again in the silver dress and translucent cloak.

"Was that a dream?" he asked, "or did it really happen?"

"It was as real as your life could be with us," Melusine explained. "You could explore the lake with us and have companionship for the rest of your life if you wish it."

"I don't know," replied John. "I'm not sure I am ready to have my life so utterly changed."

"Linnet changed her life for you, once her decision to be with you was made, she could not return to her life with us. It was hard but she never regretted it. She knew that as you were from different worlds, she would be unable to bear you a child and that that a pregnancy would be the kiss of death to her. If you choose to join us, like Linnet you would never be able to return to your old life. It is a hard decision to make and I understand that you will want to think about it for a while."

Melusine drew one of the silver hair ornaments from her blond locks and handed it to John. "If you decide to join us, throw this into the lake when the moon is full and I will return for you."

She stood and with a sad smile bade him farewell before diving into the lake, leaving only ripples on the surface.

John sat and reflected on what had happened – he could hardly believe it. Had he been so distraught that he had been dreaming? He looked down and turned Melusine's silver hair ornament in his hand – it was in the shape of three fishes shaped as a triskelion with a moonstone in the centre. He reached into his trouser pocket and withdrew a silver pendant on a chain which he had taken from his wife's neck before he buried her. It was an identical three fishes triskelion but, in place of a moonstone, it had a blue stone in the centre, the colour of Linnet's eyes.

For Jess

In the bleak greyness of a morning storm, winds whipped the waves into a frenzy as they pounded the beach and then retreated to the sea. Walking along the shoreline was a middle-aged woman accompanied by a lively jet-black dog who was racing into the waves and then returning to the woman, dancing on his paws waiting impatiently for her to throw yet another stone.

She seemed to be in her element, dressed in blue jeans, trainers and a bright red jacket covered with blue and white lighthouses – perfect for the location. This was her favourite time of year. Autumn, when the shore came alive with the sounds of the crying seagulls fighting the winds to stay aloft and the salty, grey-green sea depositing all sorts of flotsam and jetsam which she normally enjoyed picking over to find items she could recycle. Today, however, she seemed distracted, much to the disappointment of the dog who jumped at her side, barking.

Finally, the dog's barks gained her attention and, stooping to pick up a stone, she smiled. "OK Max - one last stone before we have to go in!" and with that, she threw the stone as hard as she could into the waves. Max raced after the stone, tail wagging, impervious to the cold, briny water and, on finding the stone, he returned and deposited it at her feet and sat, waiting for another throw.

"Sorry Max, time to go home," she said, and headed for a small stone cottage just beyond the beach with Max reluctantly bring up the rear. The cottage was separated from the beach by sand dunes and a small white picket fence which could have benefited from a lick of paint. Due to the saltiness of the air, only scrubby grasses grew here but this was one of the reasons why she loved the cottage – it felt like it was part of the landscape and did not detract from the wild beauty of the place.

Finally accepting that playtime was over, Max beat her to the back door and, when she caught up with him, he was busily engaged in sniffing a small parcel which had been left on the doorstep.

"What have you got there Max?" she asked, bending down to pick it up. It was a small rectangular package, wrapped in brown paper and tied with string. In block capitals, written on the front were the words 'FOR JESS'.

Jess opened the door and Max rushed in, eager to see if there was any food in his bowl, even though he had licked it clean before the morning walk. Jess followed more slowly, turning the package over in her hands and wondering who had left it there and why. She placed it on the kitchen counter and reached for an old towel to dry Max, promising him a treat if he would only sit still, but Max wriggled and squirmed as Jess tried to rub his coat dry. Wrinkling her nose at the wet dog smell now pervading her kitchen, Jess went to the cupboard to fetch him a biscuit which, although not earned, she could not refuse. Now Max sat most obediently and held out a paw before accepting the biscuit and demolishing it within seconds.

Switching on the kettle, Jess returned to the package. She carefully untied the string and unwrapped the brown paper, revealing an oblong red box. She opened the box and inside, nestled within layers of tissue paper, was a beautiful string of pearls with a gold clasp. Jess stared at the pearls. She was sure she recognised them; they had belonged to her mother. Tears began to form in her eyes as Jess sat at the kitchen table trying to remember the last time she had seen them.

Her parents, Mike and Emma, had also had a love of nature and one of their favourite pastimes was to walk on the beach, hand in hand, delighting in the everchanging landscape of the beach, the sea and the sky, and the ever-present raucous seagulls, crying like lost souls. As a child, Jess had loved accompanying them, searching the beach to see what the sea had deposited and checking out the rock pools for small sea creatures. Claire, her sister, was less interested, always wanting them to hurry up so they could buy ice cream or hot chocolate, depending on the season.

Mike had bought the pearls for Emma on their thirtieth wedding anniversary and she had adored them, wearing them for special occasions such as birthdays and Christmas. Five years later, Mike was killed in a car accident and, devastated, Emma began wearing the pearls almost every day in remembrance of him.

Life continued much as it always had, with Jess and Emma regularly walking the beach with Max chasing the seagulls and the never-ending supply of stones thrown for him. Then, out of the blue, following a routine check-up, Emma was diagnosed with terminal cancer. They were all devastated. Emma moved in with Jess and bravely continued to live life on her terms although, as the cancer progressed, their walks on the beach became shorter and less frequent and then stopped altogether. As it became clear that Emma needed more help than Jess could give, Jess and Claire reluctantly moved Emma into a nursing home. Although Jess knew it was necessary, she felt truly guilty, knowing Emma would hate it there and she did. As it turned out, it was not to be for long, Emma died within three weeks and, when Jess and Claire went to collect her things, the pearls were nowhere to be found.

The doorbell, and Max's subsequent barking, roused Jess from her memories and, placing the lid back on the box, she went to the front door to find Claire carrying a bag of shopping.

"Hi – I've been to M&S and got you a couple of bits!" Claire exclaimed while trying to prevent Max from licking her face. "Get down your naughty dog!   You're wet and you smell!"

"Come in – I was just making a coffee," said Jess, leading the way back to the kitchen. Claire dumped her bags on the kitchen table and collapsed into the nearest chair.

"What's this?" she asked, spying the box. Jess explained how she had discovered it on the back porch step and that she thought the pearls were their mother's.

"How could that be? Do you think someone took them at the nursing home and is now feeling guilty?" Claire asked as she opened the box and took out the pearls. "I think you're right – they do look like Mum's!"

Coffee forgotten, they both speculated on how the pearls had appeared out of nowhere. The writing on the brown paper provided no clue and, as no note had been included, it was unlikely there would be a solution to the mystery.

Claire was still holding on to the pearls when she asked, "So what do we do with them now?"

Jess looked warily at her sister. "Well, they were addressed to me and you know that Mum wanted me to have them – she left you her gold watch," she said, purposefully eying Claire's wrist displaying the beautiful watch while taking the pearls from Claire and placing them back in the box.

Claire could not disagree with Jess, it was what her mother had wanted, but she had a passion for jewellery (evidenced by all the rings, bangles and earrings she was wearing) and, despite inheriting the gold watch, she desired the pearls and could not bear to leave them with Jess. *After all*, she thought, *what can mysteriously appear could also disappear.*

"Well, we'd better put this food away in the fridge!" said Claire, opening the refrigerator and finding space for the various items.

"You do that and I'll get you some money!" said Jess, heading in the direction of her bedroom to fetch her purse.

As Jess left the kitchen, Claire looked again at the pearls. Checking to make sure Jess was not returning, she snatched them up and dropped them in her coat pocket and then carefully put the lid on the box.

"Here you go – is £20 enough?" Jess asked.

"That's fine. Goodness is that the time? I have to fly!" Claire replied, picking up the empty bags and hurrying to the front door. "I'll see you soon!" she said, getting into her car. With a wave, she drove away.

Jess headed back to the kitchen and finally made herself that coffee. She opened the lid of the box once more and, taking out the pearls, fastened them around her neck, feeling the smoothness of each pearl and sensing the link to the sea.

"Thanks Mum" she whispered quietly.

As Claire was driving home, she reached into her pocket to feel the pearls. She checked her right pocket and then her left. They were not there. The only thing she found was a slip of brown paper with the words 'FOR JESS' written in block capitals.

RON COUCH

Banger and Smash
(A nonsense list poem)

I bought a car the other day.
From the tip, I have to say.
'It's a banger' said the dealer,
'there ain't no one whose gonna steal 'er!'

Not everything was working,
so, I had to do some searching;
I looked around upon the ground
and, here's a list of what I found:

A near-side wing,
a compression spring.
A windscreen wiper
and baby's diaper.
A half-smoked fag
an oily rag
plus, some bubble gum.

A steering wheel,
a petrol cap.
A rear view mirror
and, a bonnet strap
plus, a rubber bung.

With a set of wheels, more body parts,
a tank of fuel – we hope it starts.
But, now, it's up and running
and, although not shiny new,
we're going to a banger race
to see what it can do.

Gratitude

I am grateful for this person – Why?
I want to celebrate this person
and I know the reason why.

It has to be a sunny day,
in spring or summer time;
we can indeed expect
the weather to be fine.

I love this person. Why should I not?
The years sped by, now I owe a lot
and dearly want to say
I have a debt I never can repay.

Of course I'm talking of my wife;
she's been my rock throughout
our married life. So let us celebrate
and mark the day; thank her, for the life.

Fox Ventures Forth

It was late August, dawn was breaking and the sun was rising from its nocturnal slumber; its burning brightness stealing over the tops of the low-lying hedges, crisscrossing the farmland below. A thin, ethereal layer of mist hovered, barely above the ground, scattering the sun's light in diverse confusion over the stubble of recently cut wheat.

Deep in his den, Fox stirred. The sunlight had managed to filter into to the very depths of his secret sanctum, snugly concealed beneath the roots of the hazel hedge bordering the west end of the field. He languidly opened one eye, observing the intrusive light with faint interest and scratched an itch behind his right ear. He wondered why he used his rear paw to do this; after all, wasn't his front paw closer to his head? He reluctantly opened the other eye, then climbed unhurriedly to his feet. He paused. *What's the rush?* he thought. There was nothing to rush for; he was, after all, his own master, was he not?

However, that did not alter the fact that last night's sortie to the local chicken farm saw him coming away with an empty belly. The owner of the farm had pulled a fast one and had improved the coop's defences and that had been enough to fool him. But not next time, he vowed. He would have persevered, but in his efforts to get beneath the heavy boards, placed there by the farmer, he managed to spook the chickens and, within moments, a shaft of light exploded from an opened door only yards from where he was excavating at the bottom of the coop. Framed in the doorway was the now alerted farmer, shotgun in hand, ready to blast him into oblivion. But Fox was smart; he didn't hang around and made it, hot-foot, back to his den.

Now, Fox was near starving; he needed a new strategy. He lay down again, better to think about what to do next...

He decided, at last, to give it one more go; the early morning mist still lingered and would provide a measure of cover for his next clandestine activity. He had been alone since the spring of that year; a young vixen who'd caught his eye at the time wasn't receptive and, as he was far removed from his own patch, he let it lie. He had lived the life of a bachelor ever since. But he longed for company and determined that he would, one day, seek out the young vixen and try again. Now however, there was work to be done; no time for reminiscing – the mist would be dispersing and his cover would be gone.

He made his way to the entrance of the den and, after a quick recce, slipped out into the field. Keeping to the hedgerow to better conceal his presence, he made his way, once again, to the chicken farm. He'd made good progress; the window of opportunity would soon be closed and that had spurred him on.

He arrived a touch breathless, but approached the coop with extreme caution not daring, this time, to spook the chickens. It was still early, but now the sun was higher. A stillness filled the air; everything was eerily quiet. But, what's this? Fox stopped dead in his tracks, his nostrils twitching. There were clear signs of 'others' at large. Who could that be? He drew closer – he was now oddly conscious that his paws were soaked with dew – inspected the coop and saw, in the diffused light, that something had been attacking the wire mesh itself and, indeed, had managed to breach it. Then he saw them; two sleek, grey shapes, tails as long as their bodies, moving carefully towards the closed hatchway to the nesting boxes. It had no doubt been their diamond-hard incisors which had made short work of the wire mesh – the same mesh Fox had attempted to get under on his earlier, aborted mission.

Suddenly they stopped; they had caught Fox's scent and immediately panicked. Fox saw his chance. The only way the rodents could escape was via the way they had broken in. But, such was their panic, the creatures had abandoned all caution. Fox was on it in a flash and, as one emerged from the hole they had created, SNAP, and SNAP again as Fox dispatched them with practised aplomb.

Better than nothing, he thought. *These will do for now; at least I shall sleep well tonight.*

Gathering their tails in his jaws and throwing the carcasses over his shoulder he made the top of the nearby dry-stone wall in a bound, dropped down on the far side and loped off towards his den. He stopped after a while to bury one of his catches. *I'll come back for that tomorrow,* he decided.

On a previous trip to the coop, Fox had stayed for a long time; hiding beneath the wild bramble atop of the nearby dry-stone wall. From this vantage point he had watched the hens as they grazed in the enclosure attached to the nesting shed. He had noticed and became particularly interested in one of the hens: large, full-bodied and sporting the most glorious golden plumage. *That's for me,* he had mused. The opportunity, however, had yet to present itself.

After several days had passed, Fox was again getting hungry. His impromptu larder was bare; the other catch had long since been unearthed and consumed. He decided to venture on yet another visit to the chicken farm. To his utter dismay the coop, for whatever reason, had been moved closer to the farm buildings; he had failed to notice that the whole contraption was on wheels! He was getting desperate – where else could he expect to get such pickings?

It was then, as he headed back towards his den, that he caught a glimpse of the unmistakable brush of another fox. Who could this be? A rival for his territory? An aggressive intruder? The brush became a body and with it came the head and, to his surprise, delight and astonishment, out came the vixen whom, since late spring, he'd dreamt about seeing again.

She was clearly interested this time; why else would she be so far from her usual haunts? Not too keen to show his interest, Fox moved cautiously towards her. She did not run, indeed, she came closer and proceeded to rub her neck on his.

Hmm, he thought. *'Goldie' will have to wait!*

CANDICE JONES

The Dandelion Clock

Splash bang, teasels and weasels,
Tinker tailor, I spy measles,
Dandelion clock, tick tock,
Where I'm heading is where you're not.
Bright spark, in the park,
Fly away, and make your mark,
Carrying your little seed;
Make the gardener call you 'Weed'.
Spick spock, join the daisy
In the lawns, and drive men crazy.
Sun yourself, between the blades,
Scattered, in sun-dappled glades.
Even though you might annoy,
To me you are the greatest toy.
Watch you floating in the air:
Sprite, with never earthly care.
So off you go, with a bang.
In the air, I see you hang.

Sunday Morning
Global Warning

With the ticking of the clock,
Water's rising in the dock.
Water's coming up the beach.
Soon your life will be in reach.
With the rising of the tide,
There will be no place to hide.
Soon, we shall no more pretend
That our neighbour is our friend,
As we fight for resources
From the cleaner water courses,
And we run out of food –
Then, we find the mood
Turns to one of general panic,
And it feels like the Titanic
To be stuck on this Earth,
When we find a dearth
Of the requisites for life,
Every nation is in strife,
And we see that the sea's
Full of struggling refugees.

Then, finally we will know
That there's no place left to go.

Pathetically we'll send
Out a spaceship at
The End.

GISELLE MARKS

Winter Haibun

Ice crystals, semi-translucent, grow in the sky. I shiver beneath the freezing, biting drizzle over a mean grey sea. Wrapping tightly in my winter coat, the wind drags the hems up and around. Low level sun blurring over the horizon tries to shine but is swallowed by looming cloud. The sea crashes on the breakwater, ozone and seaweed impregnate the air. Sky and sea merge into one large grey tableau with the icy sleet transforming into snowflakes. They camouflage the heavens against the fuming froth of the ocean.

Grey cold – wintry clouds
Land enfolded with soft snow
White icing blossoms

Capture the moonlight

You must capture the moonlight in a jar
Time will let you travel and take you far
Bespell the air, the wind and the water
Within the night you will trap the moon's light.

On a windless night to a shiny sea
Chanting your raptures with radiancy
Turn the moon beam into a luscious flow
Hold it so tightly so it cannot go.

Store it carefully where it can't escape
Carry it outside with dignified grace
Pour it over sanctified hands so thin
Let it sink deeply down within your skin.

Move inside the dark and let liquid glow
Reach into nature's beauty as you go
Heal sickness, destroy decay, create life
Excise the evil with the moonlight knife.

Garnet Symphony

Raspberries and cranberries, sugary sweet
Melted chocolate flowing out to the street
Mellow brass brazenly haunting my mind
Bejewelled ribbons link as they remind
Silken soft velvets brushing over skin
Thoughts whisper lazily as they spin
Sultry, sweaty limbs – we were so bad!
Delicious memories, merry and glad
Blousy roses, petals scenting the air
Wintry breezes, feathering my hair
Remembrances poignant, full of tears
Welcoming them in and banishing fears.

JAYA MARTIN

Happiness – a five senses poem

Happiness is rainbow-coloured
It smells like newly mowed grass,
It tastes like Mum's cooking,
It sounds like children's laughter,
It feels like arriving home.

The Hunchback and the Faerie Princess

There once lived a hunchbacked young man called Gob. His deformity was so bad that he was almost bent double. He wasn't the best looking of men with his straggly straw-like hair, a crooked nose, slit eyes and bushy eyebrows. To make matters even worse, his face was covered with unsightly warts. People stared at him openly and whispered behind his back. This made him very shy which in turn made him friendless.

An old farmer by the name of Rodrick took him on to work for him. Whether it was out of pity or whether it was really cheap to employ him, it wasn't known. Working for Rodrick wasn't easy. Gob had to work day and night, cleaning, cooking, doing all the washing up, growing vegetables in the little plot behind Rodrick's old dilapidated cottage, taking care of the chickens in the coop, feeding the cow and milking it daily. He did all these chores for only a meagre meal per day. But he didn't complain. The job provided a roof over his head and a bed to sleep in at night. And that was enough for him.

One fateful full moon night, as Gob was getting ready to sleep in his tiny room in the attic, he noticed a figure walking towards the cottage. Gob squinted as much as his slit eyes enabled him to and studied the figure walking steadily and purposefully towards the cottage. It was Rodrick and he was carrying something white and luminous under his arm. Gob lay awake on his bed for he couldn't help wondering why the farmer was out so late in the night and what was the thing he carried under his arms.

Just before daybreak the next morning, as Gob was getting breakfast ready for Rodrick, he noticed two figures approaching the cottage. As they came closer, Gob realised that one of them was Rodrick. And treading on his heels was a young girl. She was slightly built and was wearing a long white flowing gown

Rodrick took the girl to the little shed in the back garden and shoved her inside. Then he locked the door to the shed and walked to the cottage the key dangling from his gnarled, bony fingers.

'Now Gob,' Rodrick said as he sat at the wooden dining table and started slicing the loaf of bread on the bread board. 'We have a guest in the shed. This is her breakfast. Give it to her with a tumbler of water. Put a chamber pot in the shed for her. Make sure you clean the chamber pot daily when you bring her the food in the mornings.'

Gob placed the thin slice of bread on a plate and filled a tumbler with water from the jug.

'And Gob?' Rodrick's stern voice made Gob jump. 'You're not to talk to the girl. Not a word. Not even a whisper. I'll know if you did. And you'll be punished severely.'

Gob nodded.

'Here's the key to the shed,' Rodrick placed the key on the table. 'Make sure you lock the door after you. And hang the key on the key holder when you're done.'

When Gob opened the door to the shed, he found the girl huddled in the corner, her head nestled in her arms resting on her drawn up knees. She looked up when Gob entered, making him stand rooted to the floor. Hers was the most enchanting face he had ever seen. Her long blonde hair glowed in the morning sun light streaming through the little windows. Her eyes were huge and blue like the summer sky. But they were tear-drowned and so sad.

Gob hobbled closer and she flinched away. Who was she? Why was she here? There were so many questions he wanted to ask but what if the old farmer was watching him unseen? He was a tricky old man and couldn't be trusted. Gob left the plate of bread and the tumbler of water on the floor in front of the girl before locking the door after him.

This routine went on for almost a month. The girl didn't stop crying. She tried to talk with Gob but Gob knew that they were being watched so he didn't respond.

Then one morning, Rodrick announced that he was going away for a night of days. He warned Gob to take good care of the farm and their guest. After he made sure that Rodrick had indeed left for the village which was half a day's walk away from the farm, Gob rushed to the shed.

'The farmer is not here,' Gob told the girl. 'We can talk now. My name is Gob. Tell me who you are and why you are here.'

'I'm a Faerie princess,' the girl began. 'My name is Lula. My mother the Faerie queen and other Faeries like us live in the heaven above the clouds. Every full moon night we descend to earth to swim in the river not far from here. We remove our wings and hide them away. Without our wings we lose our magic and become normal human beings. We cannot fly back to heaven. When we're ready to fly back home we put our wings on.'

'Did you lose your wings?' Gob asked.

'Yes,' Lula's lovely eyes filled with tears. 'My mother and the other Faeries had to leave me behind. Luckily the old farmer rescued me and brought me here.'

'How did you lose your wings?' Gob asked.

'I don't know,' Lula said. 'I hid them under the gauze bush as usual before I went to swim in the river. But I couldn't find them when it was time for us to fly back. I looked everywhere. The other Faeries helped me search as well until it was time for them to fly back. They cannot stay on earth after sunrise. My mother the Queen promised me she'll look for me the next time they are down on earth.'

'Maybe someone stole your wings,' Gob said. 'Feathers from Faerie wings fetch a very good price for they're rare and magical.'

'There is a secret magic spell that protects a Faerie's wings. No one can pluck the feathers off the wings,' Lula said. 'A Faerie must give it freely and wholeheartedly as a gift. Please help me find my wings Gob. I will die here if I don't go back to my home soon.'

'I'll do what I can,' Gob got up to leave the shed.

As he walked back to the cottage deep in thought, Gob remembered seeing Rodrick carrying something under his arm when he returned on that night almost a month ago. Gob was convinced that they were Lula's wings. But where were they hidden?

Gob looked everywhere for Lula's wings. Finally, he went into Rodrick's room. There was a wooden chest tucked away under Rodrick's bed. He knelt down and pulled the chest out. It was locked. Rodrick probably took the key with him. Gob thought of breaking the lock with a hard rock or something. But he knew didn't have the strength.

He sat on the floor staring at the chest. The sun was setting outside. He must act quickly. Then out from the deep recesses of his befuddled mind a memory came to him. Years ago, when Gob first came to live in the farm, he had encountered a garden gnome caught in a trap. Gnomes were nasty creatures. This gnome looked nastier than any creature Gob had encountered. But the little creature was in pain. Gob took pity and released the gnome from the trap.

'You're stupid to release me,' the ungrateful gnome said. 'It's well known that gnomes bite the hands that feed them. Our bites are vicious and at times poisonous. But you already have such bad luck with your hunchback and ugly face. So, I won't bite you. Instead I'll give you something.'

The gnome reached deep into his pocket and pulled out a little parcel. He gave it to Gob, bowed a little and ran away speedily. Gob stared at the parcel. There where some words scribbled on it.

"DO NOT OPEN". What was the use of giving a gift that shouldn't be opened? It was a cruel joke only gnomes would play. Gob was about to fling it away when he spotted something written at the back of the parcel in tiny letters.

"But you can make a wish and risk opening. The contents may help you or hurt you. The choice is yours".

Gob shot up to his feet now and rushed to his room. He rummaged through his little cloth bag which contained his only belongings. His hand touched the parcel tucked away deep inside the bag. He pulled it out and sat on his bed staring at it.

"DO NOT OPEN". The words bold and dark written on the parcel loomed at him. He closed his eyes and thought.

'Please let it be the key to open the chest. I only want to help Lula.'

Then suddenly the parcel felt heavy. There was something hard inside. He felt it again. His fingers found something that resembled a key head. He tore the parcel open immediately. Something dropped out and landed with a clunk on the floor. It was a key.

Gob picked the key up and rushed to Rodrick's room as fast as his hunchbacked body would allow him. With shaky hands he tried opening the old lock. Click. It opened. With bated breath, Gob opened the chest. He rummaged through the clothes and stuff. Then his fingers found something feathery. He removed the clothes and there at the bottom of the chest lay a pair of wings, white and luminous.

With the wings secure in his hands, he hobbled to the kitchen to retrieve the key to shed. But the key was gone. Gob tottered as fast as he could to the shed. It was open. Rodrick was pulling poor Lula out of the shed. Now what was Gob going to do? He couldn't fight Rodrick with his hunchbacked body. So he hid Lula's wings under some bushes behind the chicken coop and then dragged himself to confront Rodrick. He hadn't a clue how he was going to safe Lula but try he must.

'There you are Gob,' Rodrick said. 'Now look after the girl for me. I need to take something from the cottage. I'm going to be rich Gob. Filthy rich. Then you can have two warm meals a day.'

Rodrick handed Lula to Gob after warning him to stay put and not go anywhere. He then did a little jig before he half ran half walked to the cottage.

'Come,' Gob whispered to Lula. 'I found your wings.'
He pulled Lula to the bushes where he had hidden her wings. All the while he kept glancing at the cottage lest Rodrick came back and caught him helping Lula escape.

'My wings,' Lula gasped with delight as she picked up the luminous wings and put them on.

Just then a scream full of rage reached Gob's ears.

'Quickly,' he told Lula. 'Fly away. Go now to safety.'

'But what about you?' Lula hesitated. 'The old farmer will punish you. Look he is running out of the cottage. He has spotted us.'

'Go now,' Gob urged. 'Fly away princess.'

'Come with me.' Lula said as she held out her hand.

'I'll get you,' Gob heard Rodrick's threatening voice full of fury. 'I'll kill you.'

Gob grabbed Lula's hand and instantly his feet left the ground. They were flying, flying away from the farm, away from the angry old farmer, away to safety.

When they reached the river it was almost daybreak and the faeries were getting ready to fly back to heaven. Then a tall faerie with long golden hair like Lula's come rushing forward to envelop Lula in her arms.

'Thank you,' she told Gob in her sweet melodious voice. 'Lula tells me you risked your life to save her.'

Gob felt himself blushing. There were so many beautiful faeries at the river and all their attention was on him now. He became acutely aware of his hunch back and wart covered face.

'As a reward for you kindness and bravery I grant you a wish Gob,' The Faerie Queen told him. 'You can choose to have either wisdom of the mind and generosity of the heart or beauty of face and strength of body. You must make your choice quickly. The sun is rising and we must leave soon.'

Gob gazed down at his deformed self. His hand touched his wart covered face.

'I choose wisdom and generosity,' Gob said.

'Are you sure Gob?' The Queen asked.

'I want to be beautiful and strong, yes,' Gob said. 'But beauty and strength don't last forever. I will one day grow old and lose my beauty and strength. That's the law of nature. Wisdom and generosity however, will be with me until I die.'

'Excellent choice,' the Queen smiled serenely. 'Your wish is granted Gob. You will always be wise and generous.'

'Thank you.,' Gob bowed as best he could with his hunchbacked body.

'Now, I have a wish of my own to grant to you for saving my daughter,' the Queen said. 'It is my wish that you have beauty of face and strength of body.'

Gob gasped. His body was straightening. He heard surprised whispers and cheers as he now stood tall and straight with broad shoulders and slim waist. He touched his face tentatively. His skin felt smooth and his nose was no longer crooked.

'And this is my gift to you for all your help and for risking your own life to safe me,' Lula plucked a feather from her wings and handed it to him. 'Sell it to the highest bidder. It'll bring you enormous wealth that will last till you die.'

With that the faeries bid Gob good bye as the sun slowly began to ascend in the sky. Gob walked to the village away from Rodrick's farm. He couldn't believe what had just happened. But the beautiful luminous feather in his hand proved everything that had happened was indeed true. He was now strong enough to work for a better living. So, would he sell the Faerie feather that reminded him of beautiful Lula the Faerie princess?

ANNA MERCER

360 Degree Vision

Glistening eyes
I rotate my world to encompass it all
Sliding in every direction
My vision is circular
Undulating in every dimension
Like the Sun

I lie on the Earth
The Sky invites me
I fly inside myself
The Sun glitters, and I burn

I am so cold, burning alone
Shining in my multi-directional orbit
Like a lunatic Star
I enfold the long-suffering Earth
And dry her tears

Familiar

When the night falls, I RISE
And many layers of dream
Uncurl from the coil about my skull
And dance before my eyes

Poison flowers, black, blue and red
Crack the concrete slabs of grey
And with my blood the child is fed
To do my work the Familiar way

Skin-flower

So – your skin dies
Pulled into darkness
Send me into hell
Along with sacrifices

Punish me when I am weak
When I don't know how to speak
I'll bury your dead skin and blood
And recreate your form in mud

LITTLE SKIN-FLOWER, DO MY WILL
SITTING ON THE WINDOWSILL
I HAVE LENT YOU HAIR AND NAIL
SO YOU CAN GO WHERE DEMONS FAIL

Go to him whose form you take
Slowly make his spirit break
Show him what it's like to see
Your mind contract in agony

CHRISTINE POLLARD

Night Sky

Number of stars incalculable
innumerable pricks of light
going back millennia
heavenly bodies up on high
there to see in all their glory
showing us their amazing display
knowing the constellations and planets
yearning for so many more to see.

                    The mighty spectacle of the moon
          Beyond appears orion, the ursas and gemini
                        Our eyes forever exploring
                        Drawn to the arc up high
                   As if the roof of a mighty tent
                      Lighting our endless skies
                 With silver amid the inky black
                 'Til morning creeps in stealthily

GRAINNEY SHEARD

South Barrule in Winter

I sit above sea and under cloud,
I rule all that clings to earth,
Where mortals dwell.

The land opens up before me like a flower in bloom,
Rolling toward the sea, a kingdom of views.
And I am shrouded in a frosted cloak of mystery.

Powder snow covers all that it touches,
A patchwork of ivory, silver and alabaster,
Draping the countryside like dust sheets in an unused room.

I am beautifully concealed,
My true character silenced,
In the shadow months.

Crystal citadels appear around me, glistening with sinister beauty.
Fleeting ice towers that already shrink and melt away,
New life is just around the corner.

People walk upon me wrapped up like presents.
Rosy cheeked, robin-red, puffing, panting,
Shining with pride as they reach my crown.
Basking in the glory of their hard-won battle,
With the steep contours of my body.

I am a collector of stories,
They laugh, cry and wonder,
I long to be a part of them,
But I am only witness.

GILL STEPHENS

Message from our sea

Sea receding,
Leaves me reading
scribbles in the sand.
The beach arranged,
the words are strange.
Small stones punctuate the sounds.
A message to the land.

Devastation of the ocean.
Crustaceans full of plastic beads.
Discarded bags and water bottles,
of which we had no need.
It's immoral, dying coral
bleached by acid seas.
Money makers, greedy takers
Climate denying, planet dying
Message from our sea

Shift

Stillness awakens me.
Memories break free,
notches on the doorpost.
Murmurings hover in the air,
dissolving the night.
Clear light pours in,
Mosaic shadows shift;
mist, escaped from the wind.
Smell of sunburnt grass.
Sky reflecting patches of moss and water,
borrowed scenery, cut off by the incoming tide.
One wrong turn and you are lost

Night sky

Nowhere could better showcase stars.
I see in these dark skies timeless, shining beauty.
Go into the countryside. In our velvet night
Have the chance to catch the northern lights.
Together we can dream and watch.

Soon will come the lighter summer nights.
Knowing this, makes us grateful for winter.
You are blessed to be living on the Isle of Man

DEBRA TRACEY

Don't Look

Don't look at this short, fat woman. She's tired. She's old. She doesn't want you to see the crags and crevasses that the years have etched into her skin: the rolling hills of flesh that the copious chocolate-laden rituals of self-abuse, washed down with endless coffee and wine, have left behind.

Look deeper. Look at the family and friends, the cats, the dogs, guinea pigs and rabbits that have been loved – that are loved – by her.

Look at the joy in her heart at the kiss, stolen by the giraffe at the zoo; the breath, caught in her throat as the eagle landed on her cousin's hand at his wedding.

See, instead, the woman who is moved by the beauty of the seasons of the sea – re-creating the teal, azure and indigo hues in glass – who creates purple and gold likenesses of heather and cushag, memories to share, of the Point of Ayre.

Delight in birds laughing, chatting and sharing arias around you, the way that she hears birdsong.

Feel the peace with her as she walks along the beach on a balmy evening, the moonshine strewing jewels of sea-glass and shells before her, like rose petals before a bride – filling her heart with hope and desire. Or her thrill at the spectacle of a staggeringly beautiful mobile-like cloudy sky on a day filled with sunshine, where the smell of freshly cut grass and nostril-cleansing ozone takes her on a journey of quiet.

Waterfalls

The world speeds past, watching but not seeing as I
drown in a waterfall of expectations. I manage to free
my head into the air, just long enough to gulp it down.
And smile so as not to bring attention to myself. So as
not to admit I am not the same.

I admit
I am different

I am me

My Flaunys Isle

Finally. I am home. Here on the land I have wanted to reclaim for such a long time: waiting, yearning, the tearing away of the calendar months, decorated with images of greens and golds, purples and blues, aquas and white crashing waves. My land, whose star-rich skies hold me together.

In hope
In fear
In love

Flaunys – a Manx word meaning heaven; a place of felicity, bliss, or happiness beyond the conception of mortal man.

Get happy at The Hub

To find out more about creative writing for wellbeing at The Hub, get in touch with Janet Lees on 07624 470941 or jpx10@mac.com – and find us at facebook.com/HubCreativity

There are many more activities you can join in with at The Hub – art, craft, jogging, yoga, friendly bridge, mahjong, chair-based exercises, meditation...the list keeps growing.

To find out more, contact Janet Bridle on 01624 838180, email admin@hubclubsci.im, visit www.hubclubsci.im, or call in at The Hub, Thie Rosien, Castletown Road, Port Erin.

www.ingramcontent.com/pod-product-compliance
Lightning Source LLC
Chambersburg PA
CBHW030519130626
46549CB00007B/3061